CANADA

Janice Hamilton

Lerner Publications Company • Minneapolis

Lerner Publications Company
A division of Lerner Publishing Group, Inc.
241 First Avenue North
Minneapolis, MN 55401 U.S.A.

Website address: www.lernerbooks.com

Library of Congress Cataloging-in-Publication Data

Hamilton, Janice.
    Canada / by Janice Hamilton.
        p.   cm. — (Country explorers)
    Includes index.
    ISBN-13: 978–0–8225–7128–5 (lib. bdg. : alk. paper) 1. Canada—Juvenile literature. I. Title.
    F1008.2.H25 2008
    971—dc22   2006031668

Manufactured in the United States of America
1 2 3 4 5 6 – JR – 13 12 11 10 09 08

Table of Contents

Welcome!

Canada is a huge country. It is part of the **continent** of North America. Take a look at the map. Can you name the two things that touch Canada? If you guessed water and the United States, you are right.

The Atlantic Ocean splashes Canada's eastern side. The chilly Arctic Ocean lies to the north. The Pacific Ocean washes against Canada's western shore. And the United States meets Canada's southern and northwestern borders.

Map Whiz Quiz

Trace the outline of the map on pages four and five. In the Atlantic Ocean, put an *E* for "east." Write an *S* for "south" in the United States. The *W* for "west" goes in the Pacific Ocean. At the squiggly top, put an *N* for "north." Pick out two colors—one for the United States. Use the other one for all the water around Canada.

ARCTIC
OCEAN

ATLANTIC
OCEAN

BAFFIN
ISLAND

NUNAVUT

HUDSON

BAY

NEWFOUNDLAND

YUKON
TERRITORY

LABRADOR

ALBERTA

MANITOBA

NELSON RIVER

Calgary

SASKATCHEWAN

ONTARIO

QUEBEC

BRITISH
COLUMBIA

PRINCE
EDWARD
ISLAND

PACIFIC
OCEAN

TRANS CANADA HIGHWAY

LAKE SUPERIOR

Vancouver

DETROIT RIVER

LAKE HURON

Montreal
Ottawa

Canada

Toronto

LAKE MICHIGAN

NEW
BRUNSWICK

NOVA
SCOTIA

LAKE ONTARIO

ST. CLAIR RIVER

LAKE ERIE

UNITED STATES

MILES
0   500

0   600
KILOMETERS

▲ mountains

■ plains

■ lowlands

■ Canadian shield

★ country's capital

• cities

5

From the East

Fishing villages dot Canada's eastern coast where small numbers of people live.

Peggy's Cove is a fishing village in Nova Scotia. Some people still make a living by catching and selling lobsters there.

But more Canadians live in the southeastern **lowlands** than anywhere else. Lowland farmers grow fruits and vegetables and raise chickens and cows. Much of Canada's land is on the Canadian Shield. The land is rocky and sort of flat with lots of lakes, streams, and swamps. Many dinosaur bones have been found here!

Dairy cows graze on a farm in Ontario.

Cascade Mountain towers above the town of Banff in Alberta.

To the West

Moving west from the Canadian Shield, the flat, rocky land gives way to the **Great Plains**. Cows love it here! They have lots of space to roam and plenty of grass to eat. If you keep going west, the land buckles up. You can see the giant peaks of the Western Cordillera. It is a large **mountain range**. Do not go too far west. You will end up in the Pacific Ocean!

Herds of cattle graze in the valleys of British Columbia.

Canadian farmers also grow grapes on sunny mountainsides.

9

Lots of Water

If you were to try to count all of the lakes in Canada, it would take a long time. But if you guessed two million, you would be pretty close. Some lakes are very small. Others are the perfect size for fishing and swimming. And five—called the Great Lakes—are so huge you cannot see the other side. See if you can remember their names.

Lots of lakes mean great fishing for everyone!

Beautiful ice formations line the shores of Lake Superior in winter.

Way Deep

In area, Lake Superior is the largest freshwater lake in the entire world! It is also the deepest of the Great Lakes. It is so deep that only parts of Lake Superior freeze completely in the winter.

They are Lakes Superior, Huron, Erie, Ontario, and Michigan. Canada and the United States share the Great Lakes—except for Lake Michigan. It sits only in the United States.

Weather

Brrr! Canadians bundle up in winter. Temperatures in many places can dip low. Winter brings ice and snow. It is a good thing most Canadian kids like to skate and sled.

Because Canada is so far north, summers are short. But they are usually warm and sunny. Most summer days are perfect for a hike in the mountains or for fishing and diving from a dock.

Slow Movers

In northern Canada, you will see lots of glaciers. Glaciers are huge sheets of ice. They formed because ice and snow piled up for thousands of years. Every time snow does not melt after a storm, more layers of ice build up. The glaciers creep along as they thaw and freeze every season.

The Athabasca Glacier fills this valley.

Visitors to Stay

Explorers from Europe landed long ago on Canada's shores. Soon they were followed by French and British settlers. They came to find good fishing and hunting.

European culture remains in many Canadian cities. This European-style café is in Montreal.

The Gate of Harmonious Interest welcomes visitors to Chinatown in Victoria, British Columbia.

These days, the French and British make up Canada's two biggest **ethnic groups**. Much later, people came from China, Italy, Poland, Jamaica, and Vietnam. They made new homes in Canada.

Montreal girls dress up for a South American festival.

15

First Canadians

Canada's first people did not come by ship. They walked! A strip of land used to stretch from the continent of Asia to North America. Thousands of years ago, people used this strip as a land bridge. They crossed into Canada. They hunted, fished, and collected fruits.

An Inuit mother carries her baby in the hood of her warm coat.

In the south, they lived in houses made of tree bark or animal skins. In the north, people built houses of snow, called **igloos**. Canadian Indians and Inuits are the modern-day relatives of the earliest Canadians.

This Inuit man is making an igloo by laying blocks of snow in a spiral pattern.

These Canadian Plains Indians appear in traditional dress.

Busy Cities

Ottawa is the capital of Canada. But most Canadians live in one of three big cities — Toronto, Montreal, or Vancouver.

Dear Aunt Alice,

Today we skated on the world's longest skating rink. (I fell only a couple of times!) The skating rink is actually the Rideau Canal in Ottawa. A canal is sort of like a fake river. Rideau Canal is five miles long, so we did not skate the whole thing.

They are celebrating Winterlude here. We watched the ice-sculpting contest and dogsled races.

See you soon!

Your Fri

Your To

Anywher

Toronto is a busy city on the edge of Lake Ontario. Montreal, in the east, was built around a mountain on an island. Vancouver is right next to the Pacific Ocean. People go downtown to swim or to picnic while watching big ships sail past.

The Toronto skyline lights up at night.

People can buy fresh food and homemade maple syrup at this market in Vancouver.

Two Languages

What's for breakfast? Capitaine Crounche (Captain Crunch)! Cereal boxes in Canada are printed with both French and English words. That is because Canadians speak two **national languages**. Most people in Canada speak English. But people in the **province** of Quebec—as well as in other, smaller communities—speak and write in French. And almost all the kids in Quebec go to French *écoles,* or schools.

This bus carries students in Montreal, Quebec. Almost every sign there is written in French.

Montreal is a
large city in
the province of
Quebec.

People from Quebec are Canadians. But many of
them would like to have their own country
called—what else?—Quebec. Many Québecois
(French for "people from Quebec") are relatives
of the first French settlers. Many Canadians from
other parts of Canada are relatives of the first
English settlers. The Québecois do not want to
lose their ties to French culture and language.

This mural is in the old
part of the city of Quebec.
It shows scenes from the
history of the city.

21

Getting Around

Canadians love to drive. But with all that water in Canada, they sometimes need to take boats. A ferry is a flat boat that carries cars and people across water. Some ferry rides are short. Other trips are six hours long. You'd have time to eat lunch, read a book, and take a nap!

Can't drive across? Cars pull onto the deck of a ferry.

From Here to There

One way to travel Canada from coast to coast is by the Trans-Canada Highway. This road is 5,000 miles (8,050 kilometers) long. It goes over and under rivers and lakes. Cars cross bridges and go through tunnels to get across water. Once in a while, travelers get to take a ferry to reach the other side.

Family

Lots of Canadian families live in cities, where space is scarce. But others have homes in the country, where kids have plenty of room to play.

Vancouver is a city in British Columbia. This family climbed Cypress Mountain to get a look at the city.

24

Family Words

Here are the English and French words for family members.

English	French	Pronunciation
grandfather	grandpapa	(grahn-pah-PAH)
grandmother	grandmaman	(grahn-mah-MAHN)
father	papa	(pah-PAH)
mother	maman	(mah-MAHN)
uncle	oncle	(OHN-kluh)
aunt	tante	(TAHNT)
son	fils	(FEES)
daughter	fille	(FEE)
brother	frère	(FREHR)
sister	soeur	(SUR)

Two sisters explore a beach near Vancouver.

Fiddleheads are the young, curled-up leaves of the ostrich fern.

What Is Cooking?

Some Canadian food may sound strange. Many Canadians eat the tender shoots of ferns, called fiddleheads. Caribou meat and arctic char (a fish) are some foods on a Canadian menu. Canadian maple syrup shows up on many breakfast tables.

Shops carry buffalo and caribou meat as well as beef.

French Toast

Pure maple syrup is best served over a plate of hot French toast. Ask an adult to make you this meal some Saturday morning.

What you need:

2 eggs	maple syrup
¼ cup milk	butter or margarine
4 slices of bread	

What to do:

Break the eggs into a dish with a wide bottom. Beat the eggs with a fork. Add the milk, and beat some more. Melt butter or margarine in a frying pan. Set a slice of bread in the milk mixture, coating both sides. Put soaked bread in pan and cook until it turns golden brown. Turn it over and cook the other side. Repeat with other slices, adding butter or margarine to the pan as needed. Serve with maple syrup. Mmm, mmm, good!

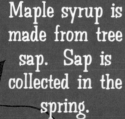

Maple syrup is made from tree sap. Sap is collected in the spring.

Schooltime

Canadian children start school when they are five years old. They learn reading, writing, math, social studies, and science. Some kids stay after school for fun activities.

Children on Baffin Island attend this junior high school. Most of the students there are Inuits.

A student practices at the National Ballet School in Toronto.

Kids might try ballet or arts and crafts. Most kids go to free public schools. But parents may pay to send their children to private schools. These may offer special programs. Either way, kids have homework.

29

Sports

She shoots! She scores! Canadians are crazy about hockey. Kids play whenever they can. They shoot the puck after school and on weekends. Indoor and outdoor rinks allow kids to play in any season. During winter, Canadians ski and snowboard. Summer means swimming, hiking, camping, and biking.

Curling

Curling became an official sport of the Winter Olympics in 1998. The object of curling is to slide a large, round stone across a narrow ice rink. The team that gets the stone closest to a circle at the end of the rink wins. Each player on the four-member team has a different job to help the stone get to the target.

Curlers slide a curling stone across the ice. The stone is a smooth granite rock with a handle attached to it.

Religions

When the French and the English came to Canada, they brought their own customs, languages, and religions. Most Canadians are Roman Catholic or Protestant.

Saint Jude's Cathedral in Iqaluit was built to look like an igloo.

Those are the main religions of France and Great Britain. But some Canadians belong to other religions too. The number of Muslims and Jews is growing. Canada's Indians and Inuits believe that all people, animals, and plants have spirits watching over them.

Holy Blossom Temple is the home of the first Jewish congregation in Ontario.

Holidays

Canadians love holidays. Whoopee! One of the biggest national holidays is Canada Day on July 1. On that day, Canadians celebrate their country's decision to make one nation out of many provinces.

Different ethnic groups show their patriotism in Canada Day parades. This Chinese dragon is from Victoria.

Quebec National Holiday

Canadians living in Quebec celebrate on June 24. This holiday used to be called Saint Jean Baptiste Day. But in 1977, it officially became the Quebec National Holiday. People proudly wave the blue and white flag of Quebec Province.

On Canada Day and most Canadian holidays, people enjoy picnics, parades, and fireworks.

A Québecois cowboy ropes a calf from horseback.

Festivals

Party down! Members of Canada's many ethnic groups celebrate their different cultures during festivals. The French Canadians of Quebec hold the world's only French **rodeo**.

Children march in the Montreal Caribbean Festival Parade.

During Gaelic Mod, Canada's Scottish people play music and have contests. The strange music of bagpipes drifts over the crowd. Meanwhile players compete to see who can throw a wooden pole the farthest. Canada's native peoples test their strength and skill during the Northern Games. They compete at drumming, pole twisting, and arm wrestling.

An Inuit man competes in pole twisting in the Northern Games.

Kiawak Ashoona is a famous Inuit artist. He lives in Cape Dorset, a town in Nunavut.

Art

Canada's scenery has moved many artists to draw and paint. But not all art is on a canvas. Many years ago, Canada's Inuit people carved tools and toys out of animal bones and animal horns. You can see some of these artifacts in museums. Modern-day Inuit artists carve figures of animals and people out of a soft rock called soapstone.

Totem Poles

Canada's native peoples are famous for their totem poles. Folks usually carve animal faces—one on top of another—into logs. Each family has its own pole. Native peoples gave meanings to certain animals. That way, people can "read" another family's pole. What animals would your family's totem pole have?

Story Time

Kids laugh out loud when they read Canadian author Robert Munsch's book, *I Have to Go!* It is a funny story about a little boy who remembers to go to the bathroom after he puts on his snowsuit.

Another Canadian writer, Paulette Bourgeois, spins tales about Franklin the Turtle. He helps kids learn how to share and how to be brave in the dark.

Robert Munsch started telling stories when he worked at a day care center.

Telling Stories

A great many years ago—before stories were written down—native peoples said the stories out loud to one another. Grandparents told them to their grandchildren. Here is one they may have told while sitting around the fire at night. It is one of the many stories of how the world began.

In the beginning, there were no people. Only one piece of land existed, and Sea Lion owned it. The rest of the world was water. Crow stole Sea Lion's baby. Crow would not give the baby back until Sea Lion gave him some sand. Crow sprinkled the sand over the water to create the world. But Crow was lonely. So he carved Man and Woman from a tree and gave them life.

Sing a Song

It is hard not to tap your toes when Raffi plays his guitar and sings. Many kids know all the words to "Big Beautiful Planet" and "Frére Jacques." Can you sing along?

Canadians like moving to the beat. They dance to country, folk, and rock and roll. If their legs get tired, Canadians sit down and listen to the **symphony** or enjoy an **opera**.

Rock musician Alanis Morissette was born in Ottawa.

Row, Row, Row

Have you ever sung songs to make a car trip seem shorter? When the French first came to Canada, they traveled long distances by canoe. To help them keep paddling, they sang song after song—loudly!

These modern people learn about Canada's history by pretending to be French traders and explorers.

THE FLAG OF CANADA

Canada's flag has a red, eleven-pointed maple leaf. It sits on a white background in the center of the flag. The maple leaf is a national symbol of the country. Vertical, red panels are on either side of the white center.

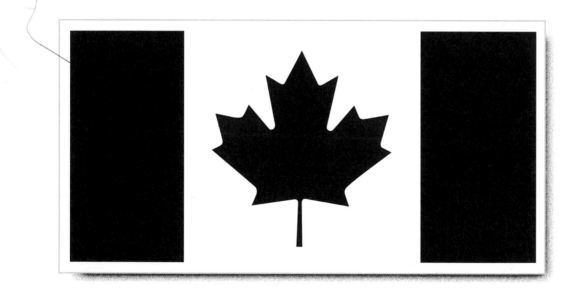

FAST FACTS

FULL COUNTRY NAME: Canada

AREA: 3,849,674 square miles (9,970,610 square kilometers), or as big as the United States plus an extra state the size of Idaho and Montana combined

MAIN LANDFORMS: Mountain ranges: Canadian Rockies, Coast Mountains (along the coast of British Columbia), and Saint Elias Mountains (in the Yukon). Canada's highest mountain: Mount Logan. Major land areas: the Interior Plateau (an area of plains, river valleys, and small mountains), the Arctic Islands (islands in the Arctic Ocean), the Interior Plains (grasslands, forests, and tundras), the Canadian Shield (low, rocky hills), the lowlands of Hudson Bay and Saint Lawrence, and the Appalachian Region (mountains, plains, forests)

MAJOR RIVERS: Churchill, Columbia, Detroit, Fraser, Hayes, Mackenzie, Nelson, Niagara, Saint Clair, Saint Lawrence, Saint Marys, Severn, Thelon, Winisk, Yukon

ANIMALS AND THEIR HABITATS: bears, deer, elk, minks, moose, mountain lions, rabbits, raccoons, squirrels, and wolves (forests); trout (mountain streams); caribou and musk oxen (tundras); arctic foxes and hares, insects, lemmings, polar bears, ptarmigan, seals, and walruses (Arctic Islands); whales (ocean)

CAPITAL CITY: Ottawa

OFFICIAL LANGUAGES: English and French

POPULATION: about 32,636,294

Glossary

continent: any one of seven large areas of land. The continents are Africa, Antarctica, Asia, Australia, Europe, North America, and South America.

ethnic groups: groups of people with many things in common, such as language, religion, and customs

igloos: shelters made from blocks of snow

lowlands: flat lands that are lower than the surrounding area

mountain range: a series, or group, of mountains—the parts of Earth's surface that rise high into the sky

national languages: languages spoken by most people of a country

opera: a play in which the actors sing instead of speak their parts

plains: large areas of flat land

province: a region within a country. Like a state, a province can make decisions for some types of activities but must follow laws that apply to the whole country.

rodeo: an event that includes contests on horseback. Rodeo events include roping calves and riding bulls.

symphony: a musical piece for large orchestra. Symphony musicians often play stringed instruments (such as violins), wind instruments (such as flutes or clarinets), brass (such as trumpets), and percussion (such as drums).

To Learn More

BOOKS

Bowers, Vivien. *Crazy about Canada: Amazing Things Kids Want to Know.* Toronto: Maple Tree Press, 2006.

Braun, Eric. *Canada in Pictures.* Minneapolis: Lerner Publications Company, 2003.

Corriveau, Danielle. *The Inuit of Canada.* Minneapolis: Lerner Publications Company, 2002.

Finley, Carol. *Art of the Far North.* Minneapolis: Lerner Publications Company, 1998.

Hughes, Susan. *Coming to Canada.* Toronto: Maple Tree Press, 2006.

WEBSITES

Time for Kids/Go Places: Canada
http://www.timeforkids.com/TFK/teachers/aw/ns/main/0,28132,537729,00.html
Visit Canada's most famous places, travel through Canadian history, and even send a postcard to a friend.

Canada for Kids
http://www.pocanticohills.org/canada/canada.htm
Visit the provinces and connect with other sites on this website developed by an elementary school in Sleepy Hollow, New York.

Confederation for Kids
http://www.collectionscanada.ca/confederation/kids/h2-1250-e.html
Learn how Canada became a country, meet famous people in Canadian history, and more.

INDEX